The Battle of Second Manassas

A Captivating Guide to the Second Battle of Bull Run, A Significant Event in the American Civil War

© Copyright 2021

All Rights Reserved. No part of this book may be reproduced in any form without permission in writing from the author. Reviewers may quote brief passages in reviews.

Disclaimer: No part of this publication may be reproduced or transmitted in any form or by any means, mechanical or electronic, including photocopying or recording, or by any information storage and retrieval system, or transmitted by email without permission in writing from the publisher.

While all attempts have been made to verify the information provided in this publication, neither the author nor the publisher assumes any responsibility for errors, omissions or contrary interpretations of the subject matter herein.

This book is for entertainment purposes only. The views expressed are those of the author alone, and should not be taken as expert instruction or commands. The reader is responsible for his or her own actions.

Adherence to all applicable laws and regulations, including international, federal, state and local laws governing professional licensing, business practices, advertising and all other aspects of doing business in the US, Canada, UK or any other jurisdiction is the sole responsibility of the purchaser or reader.

Neither the author nor the publisher assumes any responsibility or liability whatsoever on the behalf of the purchaser or reader of these materials. Any perceived slight of any individual or organization is purely unintentional.

Free Bonus from Captivating History
(Available for a Limited time)

Hi History Lovers!

Now you have a chance to join our exclusive history list so you can get your first history ebook for free as well as discounts and a potential to get more history books for free! Simply visit the link below to join.

Captivatinghistory.com/ebook

Also, make sure to follow us on Facebook, Twitter and Youtube by searching for Captivating History.

Contents

INTRODUCTION 1
CHAPTER 1 - CONTEXT OF THE SECOND BATTLE OF MANASSAS......3
CHAPTER 2 - PRELUDE TO THE SECOND BATTLE OF BULL RUN 13
CHAPTER 3 - THE BATTLE OF SECOND MANASSAS: AUGUST 28TH-29TH, 1862..21
CHAPTER 4 - THE SECOND BATTLE OF BULL RUN: AUGUST 30TH, 1862..35
CHAPTER 5 - OUTCOME OF THE BATTLE OF SECOND MANASSAS 46
CONCLUSION..50
HERE'S ANOTHER BOOK BY CAPTIVATING HISTORY THAT YOU MIGHT LIKE 53
FREE BONUS FROM CAPTIVATING HISTORY (AVAILABLE FOR A LIMITED TIME) 54
REFERENCES 55
IMAGE REFERENCES 58

Introduction

Just a little over a year after the First Battle of Manassas, which occurred on July 21st, 1861, the Second Battle of Manassas unfolded, lasting from August 28th to August 30th, 1862. Second Manassas was fought upon the original battle site in northeastern Virginia near the Bull Run River and the strategic Manassas Railroad Junction. Unlike the first occasion, the troops on both sides were more seasoned and had battle experience. Generals and soldiers alike knew more about the horrors and outcomes of war, and their arrogance had been significantly reduced from the start of the Civil War in April 1861. In the Battle of Second Manassas, also known as the Second Battle of Bull Run in the North, the number of troops was doubled, but sadly, the ensuing casualties more than quadrupled. The Battle of First Manassas was the bloodiest and most intense conflict up to that point. The Battle of Second Manassas brought the Civil War to a new record of combative destruction.

Besides fighting on the same turf, other eerie similarities linked the Battle of First Manassas to the second one. The Confederates were triumphant in both, owing mostly to poor leadership on the Union side, which resulted in poor tactical decisions. The Federal forces (another name for the Northerners or Union Army) were technically fighting on familiar ground with a far larger force, and the odds had been overwhelmingly with them at the start of the fighting on both occasions. Also, similar to the year before, the losing Federal troops, fighting in swelteringly hot summer conditions, were routed back to Washington, DC, heavily hounded by the Confederate troops. A dramatic thunderstorm ensued in the days after Second Bull Run, something which had also occurred on what was dubbed "Black Monday," which followed the Federals' failure at First Bull Run.

Both the First and Second Battles of Manassas brought Union military careers to an end, as scapegoats for the North's failure were unjustly sought out and then penalized. The Confederates watched with glee as some of the Union's best leaders were axed in retaliation for essentially making good decisions, at least in comparison to the poor ones that came from their superiors, during the Battle of Second Manassas.

Also, both battles reinforced the North's and South's resolve to obliterate the enemy. What had started as a series of skirmishes in the spring of 1861 was now evidently a serious civil war, and the ideological and economic differences at the root cause of the war turned into a permanent bloody divide that would continue until the spring of 1865.

The Battle of Second Manassas opened a gateway for the Southerners to enter previously unchartered Northern territory, bringing the war to the doorstep of the Union's capital of Washington, DC. Defeat, as well as the approaching winter of 1862, turned the Confederates home, but the Civil War would rage for a further two and a half years.

Chapter 1 – Context of the Second Battle of Manassas

The American Civil War, which lasted from April of 1861 to May of 1865, mainly began over the issue of slavery and newly elected President Abraham Lincoln's open policies toward abolition, although there were many other issues at play. Lincoln (1809–1865, in off. March 1861 until 1865) intended to end the ownership of slaves within the United States of America. The American states south of the Mason-Dixon line (devised in the 18th-century and which divided the "North" from the "South"), which relied heavily on slave labor for their plantations, conspired to break from the Union and form their own government. Although the Mason-Dixon line separated the Northern states from the South, it was originally intended to be the boundary line between Pennsylvania and Maryland. The Potomac River that runs along northeastern Virginia formed a natural border between what was to become the "North" and the "South," with the federal capital of Washington, DC (the District of Columbia), just above the Potomac in Maryland, making it extremely close to "enemy" territory.

Eventually, eleven Southern states ceded from the existing thirty-four states of the Union between December of 1860 and April of 1861 to form the Confederate States of America. These states were North and South Carolina, Mississippi, Virginia, Florida, Alabama, Georgia, Louisiana, Texas, Arkansas, and Tennessee. (In 1863, West Virginia split from Virginia to join the Union.) The Confederate capital was created in Richmond, Virginia. The North remained part of the Union government, and their people became known as the "Yankees" to the Southerners (a term that formerly referred to Americans in general). The Southern slave states formed an illegal government led by President Jefferson Davis (1808–1889, an American politician who had served two terms in the US military before acting as the president of the Confederacy from 1861 to 1865).

Although the bombing of the Federal stronghold of Fort Sumter in Charleston, South Carolina, in April of 1861 by the Southerners had been the real start of the Civil War, the Battle of First Manassas (also known as the First Battle of Manassas or the First Battle of Bull Run) was the first official land engagement of the war. The First Battle of Manassas was fought on July 21st, 1861, in which approximately seventy thousand Union and Confederate troops faced a day-long confrontation around the Bull Run River in northeastern Virginia. (The river separates Prince William County to the west and Fairfax County to the east.) The Battle of First Manassas, which was ultimately a Confederate victory, was the biggest and bloodiest battle in the United States until that point, in which approximately 4,800 men lost their lives or were wounded. The Federal troops hightailed it back to Washington in shame, and President Lincoln's war office finally realized the enormity of the task ahead and that the war with the South was going to be long, bloody, and expensive.

The area near the First Battle of Manassas remained a crucial strategic node of fighting during the Civil War because of the Manassas Railroad Junction. This junction connected the Orange and Alexandria Railroad that ran west-east toward Alexandria on the

Potomac River, which had a slave market, with Washington, DC. It also linked with the Manassas Gap Railroad, which ran northwesterly over the Blue Ridge Mountains into the Shenandoah Valley. The Shenandoah Valley was the agricultural heart for the Southerners since these fertile farmlands provided the food that was sent via the Manassas Railroad Junction to the South.

The Battle of Second Manassas is also referred to as the Battle of Groveton since there was much fighting near this hamlet, which was located about ten kilometers (six miles) northwest of Manassas Junction. Second Manassas unfolded on the west of the Bull Run River in Prince William County, extending from the Sudley Ford north along the Bull Run River to include Stony Ridge and the wooded area around Groveton to the west and then south to the crossroads around which the First Battle of Bull Run had unfolded. This crossroads was the intersection of the west-east Warrenton Turnpike that led to Centreville and crossed the Bull Run at Stone Bridge and the north-south Manassas-Sudley Springs Road. The fighting reached as far south as the Union Mills railroad crossing, ten kilometers (six miles) south downstream of Stone Bridge.

The location of the Battle of Second Manassas was within what was known as the Eastern Theater of the Civil War. This region included Washington, DC, Maryland, Virginia, Pennsylvania, and the coastal ports of North Carolina. (The Eastern Theater was one of five theaters during the Civil War. The main engagements of the war took place in the states south of the Mason-Dixon line, although fighting took place on the other side of the country as well in states like California, New Mexico, and Arizona.)

From April until July of 1862, the Federal Army, led by Major General George B. McClellan, the "Young Napoleon" (1826–1885, served two terms of service for the Union, the second during the Civil War, resigning in 1864 to run as a political opponent to Lincoln), was engaged in the Peninsula campaign as head of the main Union Army of the Potomac. This campaign was intended to be an amphibious pincer-like attack on the Confederate capital by using the two rivers that flank the Virginia Peninsula—the York and the James—to lay siege to Richmond. (The Virginia Peninsula extends from Richmond southeast toward the Atlantic Ocean.) In March of 1862, McClellan left a strong force to cover the capital but shifted a large amount of his army south to Fort Monroe on the tip of the peninsula, where the York and James Rivers met, which was about 161 kilometers (100 miles) southeast of Richmond.

In naval terms, the Peninsula campaign was a failure, but McClellan nevertheless managed to battle his way up the peninsula in a series of land engagements, eventually arriving near Richmond in late May. The Rebel troops (another name for the Southern or Confederate forces) had moved down from northern Virginia to defend the capital against McClellan, and from May 31st to June 1st, the Battle of Seven Pines (also known as the Battle of Fair Oaks or the Fair Oaks Station Battle) took place on the outskirts of Richmond. The Confederates stopped the Union from penetrating their capital, although technically, the battle was a stalemate.

During the Confederates' repulsion of the Union forces, leading Confederate General Joseph E. Johnston (1807–1891, a career soldier who served the United States from 1829 until changing allegiance to the South) was wounded and subsequently replaced by the more aggressive and tactical General in Chief Robert E. Lee (1807–1870, a career military man who served the US Army from 1829 before becoming part of the Confederate Army) in June of 1862. (Lee was one of the very patriotic US officials who agonized over joining the South and made his decision at the last moment, not wanting the war to proceed. Ironically, his military prowess would make him a powerful opponent to the North in the coming years.)

Lee and his newly reformed and renamed Army of Northern Virginia made a final repulsive onslaught of the Union forces on the Virginia Peninsula during the Seven Days Battles. The Seven Days Battles were a series of seven battles fought over seven days, which eventually drove McClellan's army back down the peninsula. These battles ended with the Battle of Malvern Hill on July 1ˢᵗ, 1862, officially ending the Peninsula campaign. (Malvern Hill lies twenty-six kilometers, or sixteen miles, southeast of Richmond near the James River.) Although tactically the Union won at Malvern Hill, McClellan ended his campaign farther down the peninsula than where he had started. Essentially, the Northerners had been repulsed.

The Seven Days Battles saw stunning casualties on both sides. Of the ninety thousand Confederates, twenty thousand were wounded, killed, or missing. Sixteen thousand Union soldiers were reported wounded, killed, or missing out of the 105,000 men who had been engaged. However, once Confederate General Robert E. Lee felt certain he had the Yankees on the backfoot and that Richmond was safe, he turned his attention to northern Virginia, beginning the northern Virginia campaign of July to September 1862 and, subsequently, the Maryland campaign (or Antietam campaign) in September of that year.

After his performance on the peninsula, General Lee reformed his Army of Northern Virginia into two major corps, commanded by James Longstreet and Stonewall Jackson, who were both crucial, well-known, and larger-than-life figures of the war. James Longstreet (1821–1904) had served the United States Army from 1842 as a major before joining the Confederacy as a general during the Civil War. (Longstreet was one of the few Southerners who rejoined the US government after the war, becoming a US diplomat.) Jonathan "Stonewall" Jackson (1824–1863) had served in the US Army since 1846, ending as a brevet major, before joining the Confederacy as a lieutenant general. He died shortly after the Second Battle of Bull Run at the Battle of Antietam after being accidentally shot by his own men and subsequently contracting pneumonia. Both Longstreet and Jackson had proved their military might during the first land engagement of the Civil War—the Battle of First Manassas—where Jackson had acquired his legendary nickname of "Stonewall" after having stood his ground against the Union in a superhuman effort of resistance on Henry House Hill.

As the northern Virginia campaign continued, General Lee sent his troops north toward the Federal capital of Washington, DC. Jackson formed the left wing, and Longstreet (known as Lee's "Old War Horse" or "Old Pete") formed the right. The Confederate cavalry unit under Major General J. E. B. Stuart was a division under Jackson. James Ewell Brown ("Jeb") Stuart (1833-1864) was a debonair cavalier who had a reputation for bravado, as well as efficiency, and he became a trusted aide to General Robert E. Lee. (Jeb rode with a crimson-lined coat and an ostrich-plumed hat that were stolen by Northern soldiers just before the Battle of Second Manassas while they tried to capture Stuart himself. Apparently, the Yankees were just as delighted to capture the man's costume as they were the man!) He was killed in action in 1864 but played a significant role in the Civil War.

Stonewall led four divisions, as well as the cavalry, three of which were under the command of Brigadier General Charles S. Winder, Major General Richard Ewell, and Major General A. P. Hill. Longstreet led five divisions north, with the leaders including Brigadier Generals Cadmus Wilcox and James L. Kemper, Major General Richard H. Anderson, Brigadier General John B. Hood, Brigadier General David R. Jones, and Brigadier General Nathan G. "Shanks" Evans.

In the meantime, the "Young Napoleon" had been trying to convince Washington that he needed the full force of the Federal Army behind him if he was to recommence an attack on Richmond. (He had sent a telegram to Washington on July 2nd stating that he had faced an army two hundred thousand men strong, which was completely untrue!) McClellan held his position on the Virginia Peninsula at Harrison's Landing, where his campaign had begun. The landing was on the northern bank of the James River, forty kilometers (twenty-five miles) southeast of Richmond and about ninety-seven kilometers (sixty miles) upstream of the open ocean. (The York River forms the northern tributary of the Virginia Peninsula and the James River the southern boundary.)

At Harrison's Landing, the Confederate Army was protected by Union gunboats positioned on the James River, but McClellan was refused his request for reinforcements. The Union government was not prepared to recall their armies for one southern campaign that would leave the capital of Washington, DC, vulnerable. Also, in the heat of summer, the threat of malaria and yellow fever from mosquitos in the wetlands of the peninsula was not worth the risk. On August 4th, 1862, the fiery McClellan was ordered to return his troops to northeastern Virginia via the James and then the Potomac Rivers.

President Lincoln had been opposed to McClellan's plan to re-attack Richmond and was more intent upon defending the Union capital, sensing that the fighting would move north from southeastern to northeastern Virginia. He was correct, and he had the foresight to appoint a new commanding general of the US Army, which had been McClellan's role until March of 1862. Major General Henry Halleck (1815-1872) assumed command of the Federal forces in July of 1862 and remained in that position until March of 1864. Halleck, also known as "Old Brains," was not only a military man but also a scholar and a lawyer. He was unpopular as a military leader and was replaced by Ulysses S. Grant (1822-1885, a military man, public administrator, and politician) who went on to lead the Union to victory in 1865 and then served as the eighteenth president of the United States from 1869 to 1877.

Lincoln also appointed one of his relatives by marriage, John Pope (1822-1892), as the commander of the newly formed Army of Virginia, which was pulled together in late June. The Army of Virginia was assembled from the remnants of other Union armies scattered throughout northern Virginia, the Shenandoah Valley, and Washington. (Eventually, the army would consist of three corps of more than fifty thousand men, but it was disbanded after the stunning failure at the Second Battle of Bull Run. On September 12th, 1862, the Army of Virginia was merged into the Army of the Potomac, never to be reconstituted.) Pope had been active in the Western Theater (specifically in Missouri and Mississippi) and had experienced successes, which led to a haughty attitude of bravado based on ignorance. He was unpopular with leaders and soldiers alike to such an extent that there was evidence of broad-based hatred against him. And his promotion by the president to commanding general of the main Union army above his superiors did not help matters!

Pope was placed in charge of the Army of Virginia in July of 1862, making himself even more unpopular, specifically with the commanding general of the South, Robert E. Lee, when he began terrorizing the civilians of northern Virginia, which was technically Southern territory that the Northerners dominated during the war. Lee labeled Pope as a "miscreant" who ought to be "suppressed," as he took food and supplies from local homesteads and threatened to execute prisoners of war, suspected traitors, and civilians alike. Pope also had a broader, politically enforced objective from his president to begin influencing the Southern civilians by using the incentive of alleviating the hardships they were experiencing as a result of the war. General Orders 5, 7, and 11 aimed to compensate food-producing farmers who were loyal to the Union, annihilate Confederate guerilla operations, and prevent civilian hostilities toward the Federals. Unfortunately, in many cases, these orders were taken too far by the Yankees, who used them as an opportunity to plunder, pillage, and punish innocent people and their property.

The 1st Corps of the Army of Virginia was led by Major General Franz Sigel (1824-1902, a German American soldier and revolutionary who recruited many German-speaking immigrants to the Federal Army), who replaced Major General John C. Frémont (1813-1890, who served three terms of service for the US Army) and had resigned in disgust upon the appointment of Pope, who was technically his junior in rank. The 2nd Corps was led by Major General

Nathaniel P. Banks (1816-1894, a politician and serviceman during the war), and the 3rd Corps was led by Major General Irvin McDowell (1818-1885, a career army officer who had been held responsible for the Northern defeat at the First Battle of Bull Run and demoted). Troops from Washington under Major General Samuel D. Sturgis formed the reserves for the Army of Virginia, and three separate cavalry brigades, under Colonel John Beardsley, Brigadier Generals John P. Hatch, and George D. Bayard, were attached to the three military corps.

McClellan was ordered to join forces in northern Virginia with Pope to form a substantial army that would be about seventy-seven thousand men strong. McClellan's addition to the Army of Virginia eventually included the Army of the Potomac's 3rd, 5th, 7th, and 9th Corps. (The 2nd and 6th Corps were promised for later since the Potomac Army would take time to move north from the peninsula.) The four Potomac corps were led by Major Generals Samuel P. Heintzelman, Fitz J. Porter, William B. Franklin, and Jesse L. Reno, respectively. One brigade of the Kanawha Division (a detachment originating from the start of the war named after a western Virginian valley) under Colonel Eliakim P. Scammon also joined with the Potomac additions, specifically at the start of Second Bull Run. Pope spread his body of men out in an arc across northern Virginia.

The right flank was positioned under Sigel on the Blue Ridge Mountains at Sperryville, Virginia, eighty kilometers (fifty miles) west of Manassas, protecting the Shenandoah Valley. The Union center was positioned a few kilometers northeast of Sperryville under Banks, and the left flank under McDowell was posted to Falmouth on the Rappahannock River, just north of Fredericksburg—halfway between Washington and Richmond. Lee, with a mere fifty-five thousand men, knew when the Army of the Potomac began withdrawing from the Virginia Peninsula and that they were on their way to join the northern forces. As the leading general of the Confederacy, he could not afford for the Union to combine forces, so he planned to intercept McClellan on his way north.

By mid-July, Jackson's men were on the move north, but Lee waited another month until mid-August, once he had received intelligence that McClellan was on the move, to send Longstreet to join Jackson. By August 15th, Lee had dispatched most of his men from Richmond to confront Pope. Lee's intention, which he repeated at the Battle of Chancellorsville of 1863, was to pin the enemy from the front using Longstreet and send Jackson to pinion their rear, thus attacking them from both ends.

Chapter 2 – Prelude to the Second Battle of Bull Run

General John Pope's main purpose was to protect the Shenandoah Valley, as well as Washington, DC, from the enemy. He also needed to protect Aquia Creek, an inlet near the mouth of the Potomac River from where he expected George McClellan's troops to arrive. Also, Pope needed to detract from McClellan's movement north of the Virginia Peninsula, so he planned to move his troops toward Gordonsville. Moving his troops was a decision counterintuitive to laying a wide defensive position across northern Virginia, but Pope was also in an impossible situation, not knowing whether to remain on the defensive or move to the offensive. Gordonsville lies approximately 160 kilometers (100 miles) southwest of Washington, DC, and 106 kilometers (66 miles) northwest of Richmond. The settlement of Culpeper, forty-five kilometers (twenty-eight miles) northeast of Gordonsville, was to become a crucial node during August of 1862. Unfortunately, Stonewall Jackson had beat Pope to Gordonsville and had occupied it with more than fourteen thousand men (possibly up to eighteen thousand men) since July 19th. (Jackson's men had arrived via railroad.)

Having decided Richmond was safe from McClellan, Confederate General Robert E. Lee dispatched most of his troops from the Southern capital. By the end of July, Jackson had been reinforced by a further ten thousand men under General A. P. Hill (1825–1865, who served the US Army from 1847 before switching allegiance to the Confederacy and who was shot dead by a Union soldier a week before surrendering to the Union). Lee's intention was to disable Pope's army before McClellan could reach him. McClellan, who did not agree with his orders from Washington to return north, delayed his removal from the peninsula until mid-August, eventually leaving a single corps behind. The Confederates had also received intelligence stating that it appeared Union Major General Ambrose Burnside (1824–1881, a soldier, politician, and industrialist who served the Federal Army from 1847 until the end of the Civil War) was moving his troops from North Carolina to join Pope. (Burnside had played an important role in the Battle of First Manassas. His 9th Corps eventually joined the action at Second Bull Run under Major General Jesse L. Reno, 1823–1862, a career officer who was tragically killed later that year in the Maryland campaign by a rookie Union soldier.)

At the end of July, Pope moved his headquarters into the field, but instead of waiting for McClellan's reinforcements, the general dispatched some of his forces to Cedar Mountain in Culpeper County, from where he could launch cavalry raids on Gordonsville. Pope sent out one brigade and one cavalry unit from Nathaniel Banks's corps to move south on August 6th. Pope intended to eventually charge on Gordonsville to capture the rail junction and to simultaneously detract from McClellan's movements north. (Cedar Mountain is thirty-two kilometers, or twenty miles, northeast of Gordonsville and sixteen kilometers, or ten miles, southwest of Culpeper.)

In response, Jackson advanced toward Culpeper on August 7th, where the central 2nd Corps of the Union Army was beginning to coalesce. Jackson's intent was to protect central Virginia by attacking the Federal vanguard and weakening Pope's army. He also intended to capture Culpeper (specifically the Union stronghold at Culpeper Court House) before the three Federal corps united. This divide and conquer tactic had proved successful in Stonewall's previous Shenandoah Valley campaign in the spring of that year, but the sweltering heatwave in early August 1862, as well as poor military instructions, ultimately did not allow Stonewall to repeat his earlier successes in northern Virginia in the same manner.

An advanced cavalry unit sent by Jackson alerted the Union to the advancing enemy. Pope immediately ordered Major General Franz Sigel's 1st Corps to march south to Culpeper, and Banks's men assumed a defensive line on a ridge above Cedar Run (Cedar Creek), eleven kilometers (seven miles) south of Culpeper Court House and just to the northwest of Cedar Mountain. The Confederates crossed the Rapidan River on the morning of August 9th and entered Culpeper County. Upon approaching the enemy on the ridge, the Battle of Cedar Mountain (also known as Slaughter's Mountain or Cedar Run) ensued, mostly as a series of intense artillery fighting until 5 p.m. that day. Confederate General Charles S. Winder (1829-1862, a career military officer) was leading the left flank division and met his end when he was badly mauled by a Union artillery shell. His replacement, as well as general confusion amongst the Confederate units, resulted in the lack of a cohesive attack plan by the Southerners. The Northerners, under Major General Nathaniel Banks, took the opportunity to attack Jackson's troops before they could advance.

A Confederate counterattack led by Major General A. P. Hill pushed Banks's troops back over Cedar Creek. Despite fighting back, by 8 p.m., the Union was in full retreat but hotly pursued and under heavy attack from the Confederates. However, Jackson's overall advance on the Northerners at Cedar Mountain was stopped by the arrival of Brigadier General James B. Ricketts (1817-1887, a career officer) of the 3rd Corps Army of Virginia, as he covered Banks's withdrawal. By 10 p.m., the determined Stonewall Jackson finally called off the chase for several reasons, most importantly because he was alerted that not only were the remainder of General Irvin McDowell's troops due to arrive but also that Sigel would soon be upon the scene.

The Confederates won the day, but Stonewall's intentions of dispatching with the Union Virginia Army piecemeal would not be realized. The Rebels fell back south of the Rapidan River to Orange Court House, thirty-one kilometers (nineteen miles) south of Culpeper. Jackson remained in position for a few more days, but realizing that the Army of Virginia was finally together, he withdrew his men to Gordonsville on August 12th. The Battle of Cedar Mountain had been the first official engagement of the northern Virginia campaign, and it effectively shifted the area of focused engagement of the Civil War from the peninsula to northern Virginia. The battle was considered a slaughter, and of the almost seventeen thousand Confederate and eight thousand Union troops that were engaged, there were approximately four thousand casualties—killed, injured, or missing. Commanding General Henry Halleck no longer felt confident in Pope's approach on Gordonsville with the wild and unpredictable Jackson still on the loose. He called off the Federal campaign, giving Robert E. Lee the upper hand to direct the following course of the war.

By mid-August, General Lee came upon the opportunity he had been looking for when he discovered Pope's Army of Virginia (sixty thousand strong) positioned in the confluence between the Rapidan and Rappahannock Rivers northwest of Fredericksburg. But on the morning of August 18th, a copy of his attack orders was stolen by a division of the Union cavalry—the same raid in which Jeb Stuart was almost captured. Pope withdrew his army out of harm's way the next day to the northern bank of the Rappahannock, but Lee continued to poke at the enemy. Four days of skirmishes, lasting from August 22nd to August 25th, ensued, but Pope held his ground. These included the

Battles of Waterloo Bridge, Lee Springs, Freeman's Ford, and White Sulphur Springs, resulting in a few hundred casualties in total.

Heavy rains had swollen the river and made it impossible for Lee to breach. General Pope knew that he had less than a week to wait for McClellan's reinforcements to arrive, potentially bringing his numbers to over 100,000 men. On the rainy night of August 22nd, Jeb Stuart's cavalry reconnoitered the area around Manassas Railroad Junction and plundered the vulnerable Catlett's Station just south of Manassas. They were unable to burn the premises because of the wet conditions, but they made quick work of taking what they could. A captured dispatch book alerted the Confederates to McClellan's imminent arrival. The pressure on General Lee to devise an alternative plan increased, and he decided to infringe upon Pope's advantageous position by cutting off the Union railroad supply line to Washington, DC.

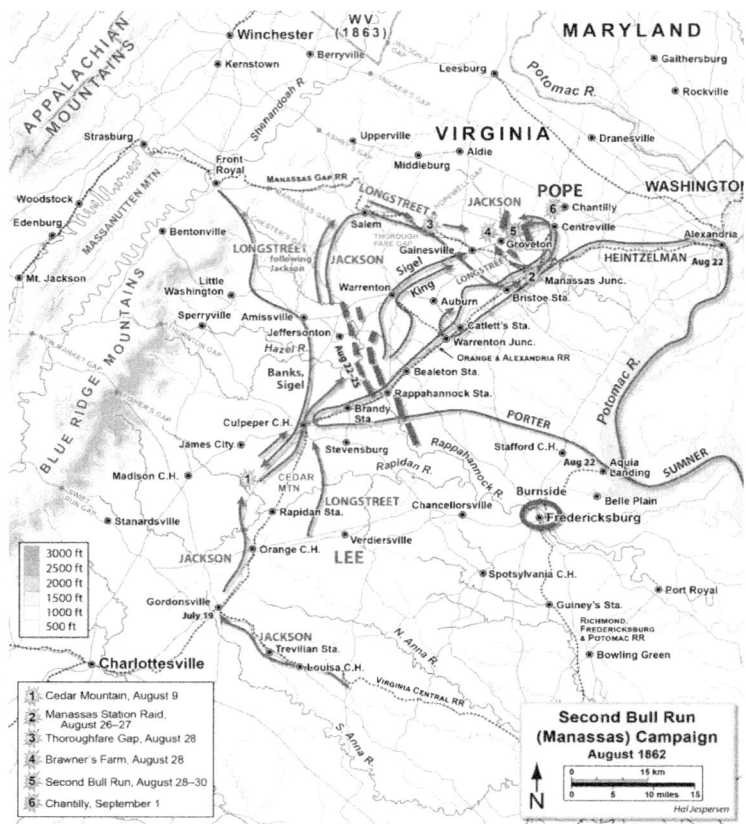

/1/ *The northern Virginia campaign of Robert E. Lee's Confederate Army during August of 1862 that led to the Battle of Second Manassas (blue for Union forces, red for Confederate).*

Lee conspired to send the intrepid Stonewall Jackson on an outlandish and daring feat north to circumnavigate the enemy in their protected position behind the river. Jackson was ordered to move beyond the enemy's front lines in a wide right flanking maneuver to the west, circling back down upon the Union's rear and effectively intercepting their clear route north, as well as cutting off crucial supply lines. Longstreet's wing was instructed to remain along the southern bank of the Rappahannock River to detract the enemy from Stonewall's movements. In the pre-dawn hours of August 25th, Stonewall Jackson's twenty-five thousand men embarked upon an eighty-seven-kilometer-long (fifty-four-mile) circling approach upon foot from the Rappahannock River, moving northwest and through the Thoroughfare Gap of the Bull Run Mountains. This loop essentially moved eastward to descend upon the Manassas Gap Railroad Junction, enclosing Pope's men within enemy territory.

It took Jackson less than forty hours to capture Bristoe Railroad Station of the Orange and Alexandria Railroad leading to Washington on August 26th. Bristoe was just five kilometers (three miles) south down the line of the most strategic rail node of the Civil War—the Manassas Gap Railroad Junction. The Confederates now held the rail link north, cutting off supplies and communication between the Yankees and their home turf. Not only was rapid communication via telegraph now stalled but so was the quick movement of all Union reinforcements south, including soldiers. Jackson's men were ordered to ransack the main Union supply depot at the Manassas Junction and burn what they couldn't steal to the ground. It was a daring and opportunistic attack, even by today's military standards. (Pope's men had previously led a raid to capture cavalry commander Jeb Stuart, who had managed to escape but left his famous cape and hat behind. These accouterments and other belongings, as well as his adjutant, were taken by the Yankees, which enraged Stuart. The cavalryman retaliated by plundering General Pope's headquarters at Catlett's Station—even farther south down the railroad—on August 22nd, making off with three hundred prisoners, $35,000 in Union payroll money, and other booty, including Pope's personal battle clothes and a copy of his attack plans!)

When General Pope received intelligence of Stonewall's infringement, he reacted immediately and chased the enemy to Manassas. Pope was emboldened by the idea of using the division in Confederate troops to first encroach upon Jackson and to then turn his attentions to Longstreet's thirty thousand men to the south. Technically, the odds of a Federal success in this maneuver were high—they outnumbered the Southerners by between one to two and one to four, depending on the military arrangements and the arrival of reinforcements.

But when Pope arrived at Manassas, the Southerners had already fled the scene, and Jackson was nowhere to be found. Reports reached Pope that the enemy planned to march upon the settlement and strategic Union stronghold of Centreville, sixteen kilometers (ten miles) northeast of the junction across the Bull Run River. Jackson had, in fact, sent out several groups in mock feints to mislead the Union scouts. Without confirming the Confederate movements, Pope marched his full army toward Centreville to obliterate an enemy he knew was considerably less in number. But like a horse blinkered by a single goal, Pope had conveniently forgotten the remaining Confederate forces under Longstreet, who had moved north following Jackson. Pope also hadn't considered that Jackson was not on the march but rather lying in wait for the opportune moment.

As evening approached on August 28th, a column of Pope's men was west of the Bull Run River, across which the Warrenton Turnpike led over Stone Bridge to Centreville. The vanguard of Northerners was nearing the Confederate forces thought to be at Centreville. But Jackson's men were ready and waiting. The Southerners had set up their fireless camps along Stony Ridge near the village of Groveton, west of the Bull Run River. Stony Ridge lay north of the Warrenton Turnpike and northwest of the crucial intersection with Sudley Road, which eventually crossed the river farther north upstream at Sudley Springs Ford. The crossroads and surrounding lands had been the scene of the Battle of First Manassas a year before. When the Federal troops marched along the Warrenton Turnpike toward Centreville, they were completely unaware of the embankment of Confederates along their left flank, who were poised for action. The Union men were walking into a trap. Stonewall issued the orders, and the Battle of Second Manassas began.

Chapter 3 – The Battle of Second Manassas: August 28th–29th, 1862

General Robert E. Lee had anticipated the unimaginative John Pope's move north to Manassas, and once the Federals moved from the Rappahannock, he sent General James Longstreet in support of Stonewall Jackson—following the same circuitous route Jackson had taken from the enemy's grounds. The combination of Longstreet's and Jackson's troops would prove essential for a Confederate victory. Meanwhile, Jackson had cunningly secured his troops amongst the woods of Stony Ridge, and on Thursday, August 28th, Pope would spend an entire day unsuccessfully seeking out the enemy that he knew was somewhere near Manassas.

The unfinished railroad of the defunct Manassas Gap Railroad Company became strategically vital to the Confederates during the Battle of Second Manassas. The unfinished railroad ran south below and parallel to the wooded rise of Stony Ridge. The grading had been prepared in the late 1850s as an independent line to join Gainesville, just west of Manassas, to Alexandria on the East Coast. Work on the railroad had been suspended before the advent of the war for financial reasons, but the ground was laid for railroad construction, leaving a long trench line, which was ideal for warfare. The section where the ground was the most excavated became known as the "Deep Cut" as a result of Second Manassas.

Jackson's shenanigans around the Bristoe and Manassas stations on Wednesday, August 27th, had not been conducted entirely without conflict. Stonewall's rearguard unit under Major General Richard S. Ewell (1817-1872, "Old Bald Head" or "Baldy," a career US army officer who joined the Confederacy and was a key figure under Lee and Jackson) was attacked by Union forces near Bristoe Station during the afternoon, in what became known as the Battle of Kettle Run. The Union unit led by Major General Joseph Hooker (1814-1879, "Fighting Joe," a career US Army officer who served three military terms for the US, including in California) had advanced from Catlett's Station along the Orange and Alexandria Railroad, searching for the Confederate miscreants. Ewell put up a strong resistance before retreating to join the bulk of Jackson's troops at Manassas Junction. There were up to six hundred casualties in the Battle of Kettle Run—killed, wounded, and missing.

Also, on the 27th, Union General George W. Taylor (1808-1862, a career military man who served one term in the US Navy and two in the US Army) of the Northern 1st New Jersey Brigade was called west from Alexandria to deal with the skirmishes that were apparently ensuing around Manassas. Upon reaching Jackson's forces near the junction and realizing the full might of the enemy, the brigade made a hasty retreat back over the railway bridge at Union Mills, south of the Warrenton Turnpike. The Confederate forces chased Taylor's men back over the bridge in a rout during what is known as the Battle of Manassas Station. Union General Taylor died four days later from a leg injury sustained that day, but he was immortalized in the poem "The General's Death" by the modern Irish poet Joseph O'Connor.

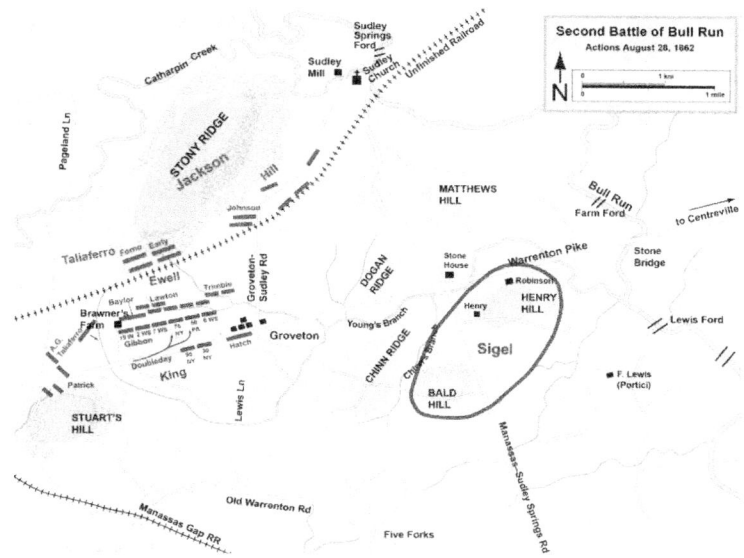

[2] Arrangement of troops at the start of the Battle of Second Manassas on the evening of Thursday, August 28th, 1862, showing the unfinished railroad below Stony Ridge (red for the Confederates and blue for the Union).

Stonewall's four divisions of men settled into the trees of Groveton Woods on Stony Ridge after they had plundered and burned all Yankee supply stations in and around Manassas Junction. Their encampments stretched from Sudley Church, where Sudley Road crossed the Bull Run River north at the Sudley Springs Ford to Groveton, three kilometers (almost two miles) to the southwest (very close to the old Manassas battlefield). Twenty-four hours later, in the early evening of Thursday the 28th, Jackson's quarry came to him when elements of Pope's army moved east toward Centreville, exposing themselves to Jackson's artillery.

The units of the Union column included those under Brevet Major General John P. Hatch (1822-1901, a career military man who led Brigadier General Rufus King's "Black Hat Brigade," who was absent due to epilepsy), such as General John Gibbon, Major General Abner Doubleday, and Brevet Major General Marsena R. Patrick. At about 6 p.m., General John Gibbon (1827-1896, a career US Army officer) was positioned around Brawner's Farm (home to the John Brawner family), south of the unfinished railroad and southwest of Stony Ridge. Gibbon was the chief of artillery for Major General McDowell, and he led the Black Hat Brigade of volunteers he had trained. (Gibbon was renowned for making them wear black hats and white leggings into battle, which his troops hated, and he awoke one morning to find his horse dressed in white leggings!)

The Black Hat Brigade was originally organized by Brigadier General Rufus King (1814–1876), who had served two terms of service with the US military, eventually resigning in 1863 because of his epileptic seizures. King had at first been responsible for the Black Hat Brigade, which was also known as the Black Hats, Iron Brigade of the West, and the King's Wisconsin Brigade. This brigade, made of the 2nd, 6th, and 7th Wisconsin Infantry Regiments, the 19th Indiana Infantry Regiment, and the 24th Michigan Infantry Regiment, was eventually incorporated into the broader division of the 1st Corps of the Army of the Potomac under King's command in March of 1862. (King had replaced McClellan in the role.) The Iron Brigade of the West fought entirely in the Eastern Theater of the Civil War, even though their members mostly heralded from states of other war theaters, particularly the Western Theater (the Midwest). This infantry brigade was renowned for its uniform dress, intense discipline, and tenacious fighting, but it also experienced the highest percentage of casualties in the war.

The Battle of Brawner's Farm began that evening as a prelude to the Second Battle of Bull Run when Jackson sent artillery fire whizzing over the heads of the Union around the turnpike. The ever-crafty and bellicose Jackson had ridden out earlier that day disguised as a farmer—much to the horror of his men—to assess the approaching enemy. Undetected, Stonewall returned to his men and announced an order to "Bring out your men, gentlemen!" The intrepid Stonewall knew he needed to draw the Union into a fight before they reached Centreville, where it was likely that the full might of the Union Army would rejoin once McClellan's men arrived on the scene.

Being an experienced artillerist, Union General Gibbon ordered a counter-fire from Battery B of the 4th US Artillery, and the crossfire had the desired effect of halting the forward movement of troops. Hatch's men were far to the front of the column, and Patrick's men at the back sought cover, leaving Gibbon and Doubleday (1819-1893, a career US Army officer who had fired the first shot at the first engagement of the Civil War at Fort Sumter) to countercharge. Gibbon sent in 430 men of the 2nd Wisconsin Regiment, thinking he was attacking Confederate Jeb Stuart's cavalry, but in fact, the Northerners approached directly at Stonewall's main veteran infantry (the 800 remaining men of the previous 2,500 who had formed Jackson's "stone wall" at the First Battle of Bull Run). Pope had informed his men that Stonewall was already at Centreville, meaning the Yankees were less than prepared for Jackson's antics.

Gibbon sent his men back through the woods to sneak up the hill in an effort to capture the Rebel cannons. They met with the enemy in a series of indecisive skirmishes, as other units joined the fight on both sides. At first, Jackson's eight hundred under Colonel William S. Baylor (1831-1862, a lawyer and soldier who served the Confederacy) fired upon them in Brawner's orchard. Then, Jackson sent in three Georgia regiments under Brigadier General Alexander R. Lawton's brigade. (Jackson circumnavigated Major General Ewell's command.) As Gibbon added his 19th Indiana and the 6th and 7th Wisconsin Regiments (also part of the Black Hats), Jackson responded by sending Brigadier General Isaac R. Trimble's brigade to support Lawton.

The foes exchanged heavy volleys of musket fire as the men loaded and reloaded their weapons without pause for two hours. Jackson sent in horse artillery under Captain John Pelham (1838-1863, a skilled artilleryman who had never served in the US Army and was killed at the Battle of Kelly's Ford in March of 1863 in Culpeper County), which fired at the enemy from ninety-one meters (one hundred yards) away. Eventually, the Federals were overwhelmed three to one (6,200 men against 2,100) and separated from the enemy by a distance of a mere 46 meters (50 yards) in places. As one line fell back, another immediately took its place and unleashed a fury of firepower.

Doubleday sent in the 56th Pennsylvania and the 76th New York Regiments, which arrived after dark but were still repulsed by the Rebels. The battle ended at about 9 p.m., with Gibbon's men retracing their steps back through the woods below the farm. The Battle at Brawner's Farm was a stand-off, and the approaching darkness ended what Gibbon referred to as "a long and continuous roll."

Jackson had made his first move against the lagging Federal column near Groveton (also referred to as the Battle of Gainesville), but the resulting skirmish was inconclusive, as King's four thousand Union forces withdrew to Manassas Junction (although, as noted above, Hatch was the one who actually commanded them during this battle). In fact, the Confederates had sustained heavy losses in the savage fight, and two division commanders, Brigadier Generals Taliaferro and Ewell, were seriously wounded. (Ewell lost his left leg as a result of the battle and was out of action for the next ten months.)

William Booth Taliaferro (1822-1898) was a legislator and Confederate general during the war, and he was one of the few Southerners who served the US government both before and after the war. Brigadier General William E. Starke (1814-1862, a businessman who joined the Confederates for the war under Stonewall Jackson but was killed later that year in the Battle of Antietam) took over from General Taliaferro. During the Battle of Brawner's Farm, one in every three soldiers had been shot. Jackson's brigade had lost 40 percent of its men (1,250 men), and Gibbon's brigade lost between a third and half (1,150 killed, wounded, captured, or missing). However, the brief battle on the evening of the 28th revealed the Southern position, which drew the Union out for a battle over the next two days, exactly what Jackson had desired.

Meanwhile, Major General Longstreet, along with General Lee, were making their way toward Stony Ridge via the Thoroughfare Gap (Chapman Mill or Beverley Mill), arriving on the afternoon of August 28th, just one day's march away from joining the remainder of the Confederate Army. The Thoroughfare Gap ran through the Bull Run Mountains, about thirteen kilometers (eight miles) northwest of Gainesville. A few days earlier, Stonewall and his men had passed unencumbered through the gap—flanking their enemy on the right—but Longstreet was met by Union General Rickett's division, which blocked the eastern end of the pass.

James B. Ricketts had been sent to forestall Longstreet while Pope dispatched with Jackson at Manassas. Longstreet's leading Confederate division under Major General D. R. Jones (1825-1863, a career soldier who served in the US Army before joining the Confederacy) fought Ricketts near Chapman Mill, which changed hands three times in this intense set of skirmishes. The 1st Georgia Regulars fought the 11th Pennsylvania Regiment in a narrow quarry trench on the hillside above the mill. But Confederate Colonel Evander Law's brigade summited Mother Leather Coat Mountain to the north of the gap, descending upon Rickett's right flank. A Confederate column also passed through Hopewell Gap several kilometers to the north, thus circumnavigating Thoroughfare and adding support to the Confederates with the high ground. By dusk, the Northerners were beaten and forced to withdraw via Gainesville toward Bristoe Station and Manassas Junction, leaving the way clear for Longstreet to join with Jackson. Longstreet's clearance of the Bull Run Mountains to join the action of Second Manassas ensured the South's victory.

At dawn on Friday, August 29th, the overconfident Pope began an assault on the Confederates, not realizing that Longstreet's men had cleared the Thoroughfare Gap and were on their way to join Jackson. Longstreet's twenty-five thousand men had begun their march that morning at 6 a.m. from the Bull Run Mountains. Pope was most concerned that the enemy would withdraw, as he erroneously believed after the Battle of Brawner's Farm, he had caught them on the backfoot in full retreat from Centreville, and he wanted to retain them in a pincer movement and force a fight, boasting that he would "bag the whole crowd." The Union spread out south of the unfinished railroad, with Ricketts on the far left, King near Groveton, and then McDowell's and Sigel's divisions spreading until Stone Bridge (technically, at that point, it was a wooden reconstruction) at the Bull Run River. Pope was positioned at Centreville, eleven kilometers (or seven miles) away, with three divisions and a fourth division northeast of Manassas Junction (south of the visual of the battle maps).

The Union general was overconfident in his belief that he commanded significantly more men than the Confederates and that the result of the battle would ultimately be a Northern victory. Pope was unaware not only of Longstreet, who would be on the scene within hours, but also of where his various units were. Pope believed McDowell and Sigel were blocking Jackson's route west over the Bull Run Mountains, whereas McDowell had been described by King's division as being "lost in the woods" somewhere near Groveton and south of the enemy. Sigel was even farther south near the turnpike intersection. In truth, all of Pope's troops were either south or east of Jackson, who was living up to his reputation as a "stonewall" and was settled and ready for battle on the 29th, free to make an escape back the way he had come through the Thoroughfare.

Jackson had sent General Jeb Stuart to round up elements of Longstreet's approaching army and position them strategically for the battle. Stonewall arranged twenty thousand of his own men along a 2.7-kilometer (1.7-mile) line to the south of Stony Ridge along the railroad grade. Two of Lawton's brigades, as well as Starke's division, were centered in the middle. Stonewall also ordered General A. P. Hill's "Light Division" to hold the Confederate left flank north toward Sudley Church near Sudley Ford of the Bull Run River, which would prove useful later that afternoon. Jackson also placed a cavalry unit, as well as a battery of horse artillery, to protect Sudley Ford from a Union crossing, which would have exposed the Confederate rear. Later that day, the Confederate artillery stopped Federal Brigadier General Orlando M. Poe's brigade after they had forded the Bull Run, although they were completely unaware that they were closing in on the enemy's rear. The Union was repulsed by heavy fire and forced to retreat, but Sudley Church was destroyed in the fighting. The Yankees made no further progress in crossing the Bull Run behind the Confederates for the remainder of Second Manassas.

On the morning of the 29th, Jackson was ready for Pope, although the Federals were in disarray. Union General Sigel's 1st Corps was used to make an initial assault on the enemy, and they formed a broad front at dawn, prepared to batter the enemy head on, reaching the front by 7 a.m. (Pope had concocted a far more complicated attack plan, but because of the arrangement of his scattered troops, the first assault ended as a frontal attack. In fact, Sigel had originally been ordered toward the enemy's left.) Sigel's men were instructed to advance and engage to ascertain the enemy's position, and by 10 a.m., the fighting was full-frontal, with the Confederates using the trench of the unfinished railroad as their protective dugout, particularly around the Deep Cut.

The Federals needed to approach the enemy up a gradual rise toward the trench until they were virtually upon the Southerners. For every Northern attack, there was a Southern counterattack. Major General Joseph Hooker's 3rd Corps and Major General Isaac Stevens's (9th Corps moved in to support Sigel (Stevens, 1818–1862, was a US Army career officer and politician who was killed shortly after in the Battle of Chantilly). To the east, men engaged in hand-to-hand combat in the woods near Sudley Road; some units became temporarily trapped behind enemy lines, and leaders of sub-divisions were killed or wounded, causing panic amongst their men. To add to the chaos, wounded men from the battle of the 28th from King's division were found after a night of suffering and needed to be removed from the battlefield. When sections of the Union fell back in disorder, the Confederates rushed forward, first with musket fire but also in personal combat, clubbing, bayoneting, and knifing their foe. The Union artillery in the south on Dogan Ridge (northwest of the Warrenton Turnpike intersection) pelted the enemy when they emerged from the woods, forcing a retreat.

However, by 12:30, the fighting had reached a stalemate. Pope arrived on the battlefield at about 1 p.m. to take command, and he deliberated whether to end the fighting altogether and retreat to Centreville since McDowell's and McClellan's troops were nowhere to be seen. When Pope received word that McDowell was close, he resumed the full-frontal attack on Jackson, sending two Union brigades toward the enemy in the afternoon to puncture the Southern line. These included Major General Samuel P. Heintzelman's 3rd Corps of the Army of the Potomac and Major General Jesse L. Reno's 9th Corps, as well as two of McDowell's divisions. (Heintzelman, 1805–1880, was a career army officer who was very prominent in the first years of the war—a World War II ship was named in his honor; Reno, 1823–1862, was a career army officer and "soldier's soldier" who fought alongside his men and was killed two weeks later at the Battle of South Mountain as part of the Maryland campaign.)

One brigade under Brigadier General Cuvier Grover (1828–1885, a US Army career officer), which was part of Hooker's division, attacked at 3 p.m., thinking they were backed by Major General Philip Kearny (1815–1862, a career army officer who died shortly after in early September at the Battle of Chantilly), although it was Stevens who held their retreat. Grover made straight for Confederate Brigadier General Edward Thomas's Georgia brigade. Like all other charges of the day, Grover's men attacked at point-blank range, followed by a bayonet charge and then hand-to-hand combat. Reinforced by two Carolina brigades, the Confederates fought back, but after clearing the woods, they were forced to retreat when exposed to Union artillery. Grover faced 350 casualties due to the charge. During the engagements of the day, the Union attacks were isolated, poorly supported or coordinated, and eventually repulsed with heavy casualties and no advancement or breakthroughs.

The two sides continued to fight across the unfinished railroad, with Pope dispatching three of his units toward the enemy, including Major General John F. Reynolds's Pennsylvania Reserves (Reynolds, 1820-1863, was a career US Army officer who played a key role in the American Civil War but was killed at the Battle of Gettysburg in 1863). The wooded battle scene made it difficult for either side to deploy artillery except toward the Union's left (the Confederate right), which included open fields between the woods and the rail grading. The right was the weakest part of the Confederate front line defense, which was held by Starke's division. Jackson added General Jubal A. Early (1816-1894, a Virginia lawyer and politician who served a prominent role as a Confederate general in the Civil War) and Colonel Henry Forno's "Louisiana Tigers" brigades to bolster Starke, as well as to form a right-flank link to Longstreet's men when they arrived. (The Louisiana Tigers started as a nickname for a small group of troops from Louisiana, but by the end of the war, the term applied to all Louisiana soldiers, as they had a reputation for fearless, hard fighting.)

While the Union attacks almost found success, it was an unsupported, piecemeal maneuver that did not have the desired result of breaking through the enemy line. The charges were repulsed as the Southerners fought back. The fighting continued all day, with it being General Pope's intention to hold Jackson in situ until the arrival of the Union 5th Corps of McClellan's army. The 5th Corps was led by General Fitz John Porter (1822-1901, a career US Army officer and highly respected by the enemy but who was constantly surrounded by controversy within his own army), whose military career would come to an end as a result of the events occurring during the Second Battle of Bull Run. Pope intended to use Porter's division to hammer at what he believed to be the right flank of Jackson's army near Groveton.

Ultimately, Pope wanted Porter to sever any possible joining of Longstreet's and Jackson's armies and to force a firm wedge between them by reaching Jackson's flank before Longstreet did. But Porter was too late. McDowell and some of his units, who had arrived on the scene, moved west with Porter from Bristoe Station. When Porter arrived with his ten thousand troops to cover the enemy's right flank, he was unexpectedly confronted with Longstreet's thirty thousand men, of which Pope was unaware, so Porter decided not to attack near Groveton. Longstreet had arrived on the morning of the 29th, just in time to join the Battle of Second Manassas, which would rage throughout that day and into the next, lasting until sundown of Saturday the 30th. (Some of Longstreet's units took longer to march from the Thoroughfare Gap, trailing in at 3 a.m. on August 30th.)

The Southern right flank was no longer at Groveton but extended far south and beyond where the Old Warrenton Road crossed the Manassas Gap Railroad. Porter and McDowell were not only outnumbered three to one but also widely separated from the remaining Federal Army, which fought mainly around Stony Ridge to the north. Jeb Stuart had also ridden out to halt the Union's right-flanking advance in a short, sharp shoot-out. Porter chose not to carry out Pope's discretionary orders to attack but held his position, subsequently defending the Union's left flank and preventing Longstreet from joining the main battle that day. McDowell moved to join Pope toward Manassas, who would only discover the arrival of Longstreet's men by 7 p.m. that evening. Unfortunately, Porter's decision not to attack later made him a convenient target for the North's loss at the Second Battle of Bull Run and led to him being unjustly court-martialed. (The specific and infamous order of Pope's on this day became known as the "Joint Order"—a contradictory set of instructions, which also included a potential overnight retreat to Centreville.)

Similarly, on the 29th, Confederate General Longstreet refused General Lee's orders to attack from his position on the right flank, stating, "The time was just not right." Longstreet was not sure of the enemy's strength and positioning. (Longstreet did, however, launch a few scouting parties that night, which resulted in brief skirmishes, to assess the enemy's positioning and strength.)

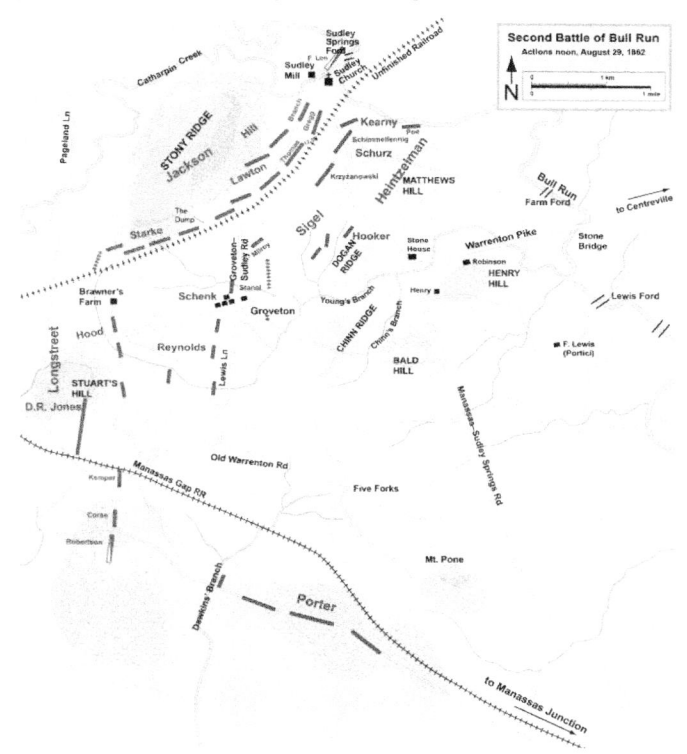

[3] Arrangement of troops at noon on Friday, August 29th, 1862, during the first day of the two-day-long Battle of Second Manassas, showing Porter's troops advancing along the railroad toward the enemy's right flank only to find Longstreet's Confederate troops reaching far south of Groveton in excessive numbers (red for the Confederacy and blue for the Union).

Tired of waiting for Porter's attack to the west that never came, by 5 p.m., Pope had sent in the fiery, one-armed Philip Kearny to assault the Southern left flank. Kearny was facing off against General Hill across the incomplete railroad. A. P. Hill was the commander of the famous "Light Division" that had found fame (or notoriety, depending on which side one was) at the Seven Days Battles during the Peninsula campaign and went on to become a significant and integral part of the Confederate fighting force. The Light Division consisted of six brigades from six Confederate states (Virginia, South Carolina, Georgia, North Carolina, Alabama, and Tennessee.) Several batteries were attached to the Light Division. The brigade had originally been a unit under Longstreet, but a feud between Hill and Longstreet resulted in the transference of the Light Division to Stonewall Jackson's jurisdiction. The Light Division had played a crucial role in the Battle of Cedar Mountain and went on to ensure a significant defense of Southern lines at Second Manassas. (The naming of the "Light Division" was first referenced in June of 1862, but its origins are unclear.)

However, the Light Division had been fighting all day for at least nine hours, and Kearny's men began beating the fatigued soldiers back. Just when it seemed that the Federals would at last break the line, Jackson advanced a reserve force into the fray, led by General Early. Early's fresh reinforcements pummeled the Federals back to their starting positions.

Despite scrambled orders on both sides to attack as dusk approached, by nightfall, the Rebels still held their position in the woods above the incomplete railroad near Groveton. Both Northern and Southern sub-commanders had rejected Pope's and Lee's ideas for advancement, citing nightfall and chaotic and clogged attack routes as inauspicious for advancement. General Pope was disgruntled that Porter had not joined the battle to the south, but he felt sure he could obliterate the enemy on Saturday the 30th and chase the Southerners from Northern territory for good. He had noted several incidents during the day that erroneously indicated to him that the Confederates were in retreat. For the third day in a row, Pope would be unaware that the (now completely reunited) Confederate Army would be waiting and prepared for a battle on the ground of their own choosing.

Chapter 4 – The Second Battle of Bull Run: August 30th, 1862

The morning of the swelteringly hot Saturday passed quietly without fighting, and Pope took the time to devise a final assault on the Confederates, who he still erroneously believed were retreating. Pope had arrived at this conclusion because both Jackson and Longstreet had pulled back, but they were simply repositioning themselves. This was especially true of Longstreet's division under Lieutenant General Richard H. Anderson, "Fighting Dick" (1821-1879, a career army officer who joined the Confederacy for the war), which was the last to arrive at the scene from the Thoroughfare Gap in the early hours of the day. Anderson's men at first advanced too far, and realizing their mistake, they pulled back west toward the remainder of the Confederate troops. This brief withdrawal reinforced Pope's mistaken beliefs. The Southerners were still stubbornly in place, despite being technically outnumbered by the Union's approximate seventy-seven thousand men (an estimated sixty-two thousand that eventually engaged) to the Confederate's approximate fifty-five thousand. A series of fruitless but incorrect reconnoiters convinced Pope that the Confederates had not moved south toward their left flank, and peculiar orders sent several of Pope's units away from the battlefield—only a few of whom returned for battle later that day.

General Lee was hoping for a fight, and besides having his united army in place and ready for battle, he had established eighteen artillery pieces under Colonel Stephen D. Lee (1833–1908, who served in the US Army for seven years as a first lieutenant before joining the Confederacy as a lieutenant general—no relation to General Robert E. Lee) above the battle site northeast of Brawner's Farm, pointed at the open fields in front of Jackson.

After much deliberation, Union General Ricketts was sent toward the enemy at noon "in pursuit" of a withdrawing army. But he shockingly met the full onslaught of Jackson's men, and after his unit was thoroughly repulsed, he reported that the Confederates were still very much present and ready for battle. Unwilling to wait for further reinforcements from McClellan that had been late in coming (specifically the 2nd and 6th Corps), Pope decided to attack. There was wide controversy around McClellan's delay in sending further reinforcements from his position near Alexandria. A letter to McClellan's wife suggested he held back his units on purpose to teach Pope a lesson and to ensure he received a whipping, thus returning the full army to McClellan after Second Manassas, which was exactly what happened. It has also been suggested that Pope moved ahead without waiting for McClellan to claim any credit of victory. These entrenched, bitter, and ongoing brawls between leaders of the Union ensured many Northern failures in the first few years of the Civil War.

After noon, Pope decided to pincer an enemy he still believed was likely to retreat. He sent Porter, Hatch, and Reynolds west toward the enemy's right flank and Ricketts, Kearny, and Hooker east toward the left flank. Porter's division, along with reinforcements from McDowell, advanced in the afternoon at about 3 p.m., with five brigades of about ten thousand men ready to strike at Brigadier General Starke's division along the unfinished railroad's Deep Cut. (They were overseen by twenty-eight artillery pieces on Dogan Ridge to defend them.) Porter's 1st Division was led by Brigadier General Daniel Adams Butterfield (1831-1901, a New York businessman and general in the Civil War). This initial assault nearly broke through the Confederates' front right center, routing the Confederate 48th Virginia Infantry Regiment. (In haste, Pope prematurely reported a breakthrough to Washington.) When the South's ammunition ran out at certain places, they, specifically the Louisiana and Virginia regiments, began hurling rocks from the unfinished railroad toward the Union troops in desperation. The Federals took the opportunity to throw the rocks back! Meanwhile, McDowell, realizing the Southerners were not withdrawing, held his position on both Bald Hill (below Chinn Ridge) and Henry House Hill.

Jackson needed to call on Longstreet for reinforcements—an unlikely move by the stalwart Stonewall. Longstreet, who was unable to move his troops toward the congested battle scene, sent forward his artillery instead under the command of Stephen D. Lee. The battery, as well as eighteen cannons, pounded the Union from the west.

Brevet Major General John P. Hatch had taken over the command of Brigadier General King, who'd fallen ill the previous evening with epileptic seizures. King's men included the Iron Brigade of the West (the Black Hats) that had been pummeled by Jackson on the evening of August 28th. The division, now officially under Hatch, joined Butterfield in the fight. (Hatch had been with McDowell and Porter the previous day as they moved up the Manassas-Gainesville Road toward Longstreet when they were set upon by Stuart.) The Union closed ranks and fought harder, but they could not withstand the Confederate firepower, and their attempts eventually stalled.

Porter, seeing the ensuing devastation, decided not to send further reinforcements to their death and called his men back to the protection of Groveton Woods. Butterfield's and Hatch's men fell back from the carnage at the Deep Cut, needing to cross open fields under a gauntlet of fire from Southern artillery before reaching the safety of Groveton Woods. They collided chaotically with reserve troops behind them, which were partially pursued by some of Starke's men, who were beaten back by the Union reserves. They had fought for an hour, and three thousand of Porter's men lay dead, dying, or missing in the field. Jackson's command, which was equally depleted, could not immediately counterattack, which allowed Porter to stabilize his men north of the turnpike.

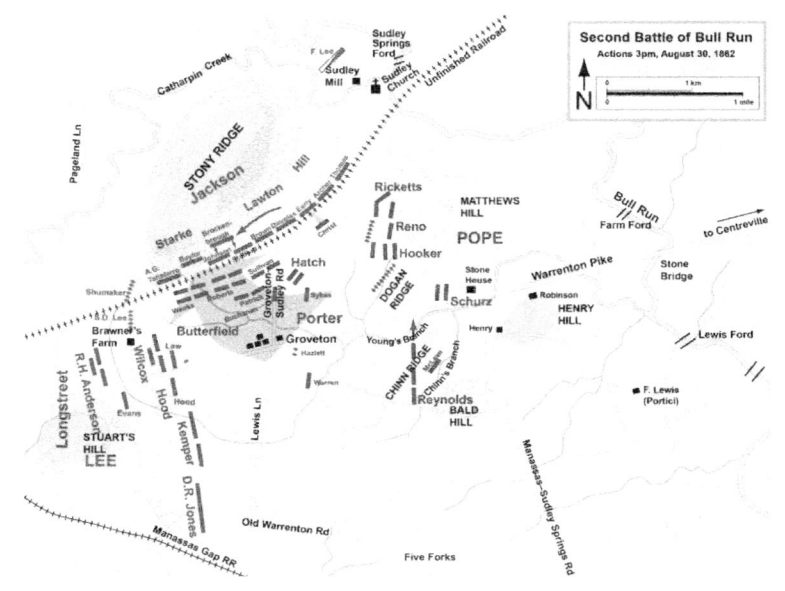

[4] Arrangement of troops at 3 p.m. on Saturday, August 30th, 1862, during the second day of the two-day-long Battle of Second Manassas, showing Porter's troops attacking at the unfinished railroad. Stephen D. Lee's battery is seen in the west (red for the Confederacy and blue for the Union).

But a full onslaught by the Yankees was exactly the move General Robert E. Lee had anticipated, and he patiently waited for the fighting to subside before launching a counterattack on the exhausted Federal troops. By holding their position overnight along the ridge and maintaining the advantage of dominating the unfinished railroad, the Confederates had managed to lure the enemy into a fight and essentially maintained not only tactically the higher ground but also the upper hand. Stonewall had once again lived up to his name by not relenting, holding the ground that determined the battlefield and ultimately dominating the line.

The general of the Union 3rd Corps, Irvin McDowell, seeing the line under Porter beginning to break down and withdraw, ordered General Reynolds north of the Warrenton Turnpike toward the enemy's left flank. (Reynolds had been positioned on Chinn Ridge, southwest of the Warrenton Turnpike and Sudley Road intersection.) McDowell's intention was to bolster the weakening troops toward the Northerners' right flank. It would prove to be a disastrous decision since Reynolds's removal left a mere 2,200 men below the turnpike. The enemy, who were thick and strong to the north and west—with the Bull Run River to the east and the railroad to the south, blocking the Northerners' escape—could now easily rout the Northerners from the battlefield, which was exactly what they did.

General Lee used the opportune moment to unleash his army and ordered Longstreet to counterattack at 4 p.m., just when Porter's men were falling back. Pope had ignored warnings of a potential counterattack, and the Union's left flank below the Warrenton Turnpike was weak and largely undefended. Longstreet had quietly decamped more than three kilometers (two miles) past the Union's southern extremities. Lee simultaneously sent Jackson to approach the Union right. The Rebels had the Federals broadly pinned against the Bull Run River. The Rebels' five divisions spread out from Brawner's Farm in the north to Manassas Gap Railroad Junction in the south, forming a wall of attack west of the north-south aligned Manassas-Sudley Springs Road.

Longstreet used the weak point below the turnpike to overwhelm the entire Federal Army, sending thirty thousand fresh troops toward Henry House Hill to halt the enemy's retreat over Bull Run. The Confederate objective was to dominate the high ground of Henry House Hill—the key location of First Manassas—in order to rout and destroy the Federals by pushing them north, as they would be unable to ford the Bull Run at Stone Bridge.

At the front of this onslaught, the Confederates outnumbered the Yankees by ten to one. General John B. Hood's Texas Brigade led the charge for the Confederates, who focused on the strategic node of Henry House Hill. (Hood, 1831-1879, a career military man who served the US Army before changing to the Confederacy during the war, was a notorious buccaneer and aggressive leader, although Texas had not been his home state but where he was posted once completing the military academy.) Hood was supported by "Shanks" Evans's South Carolinians. (Nathan George "Shanks" Evans, 1824-1868, was a career military man who served the US Army before joining the Confederacy for the war. He had played a crucial role in the Battle of First Manassas, as he'd been the first to notice the enemy encroachment from the north over the Bull Run. Dashing ahead with his barrel of whiskey, Shanks held off the enemy on Matthews Hill before the Southerners joined forces and retreated to join the full battle that ensued at Henry House Hill.)

Seeing the Rebels' plan, Porter sought out two Yankee regular brigades under Brevet Major General Robert C. Buchanan (1811-1878, a distinguished career military man who served forty years for the US Army) and Colonel Charles W. Roberts (1810-1875, a lawyer, civil engineer, and Union officer during the Civil War) to move south of the turnpike. But in the meantime, only two Federal brigades were in position to meet Hood's assault—Colonels Nathaniel C. McLean's Ohioans of Sigel's 1st Corps and Gouverneur K. Warren's of Porter's 5th Corps. McLean (1815-1905, a lawyer, farmer, and Union general during the war) held Chinn Ridge, while Warren (1830-1882, a civil engineer and Union officer) was slightly farther west (less than two kilometers or a mile).

The Confederates were at first met with Warren's two regiments of the 5th and 10th New York Zouaves. The Zouaves were an unusual unit modeled and trained in the North African Zouave mercenary style of combat, although its members were mostly firefighters from New York. The Zouaves had suffered severe casualties during the First

Battle of Manassas when they acted as a rearguard for the retreating Union Army and also as they faced Stonewall on Henry House Hill during the stand-off that garnered him his reputation. Now, once again a target for direct and brutal combat, the troops received the full onslaught of the enemy, and half of the brave and charismatic thousand-strong Zouaves fell that day within a space of ten minutes. In terms of a single infantry regiment engagement, it was the biggest loss of life within a unit during the entire Civil War.

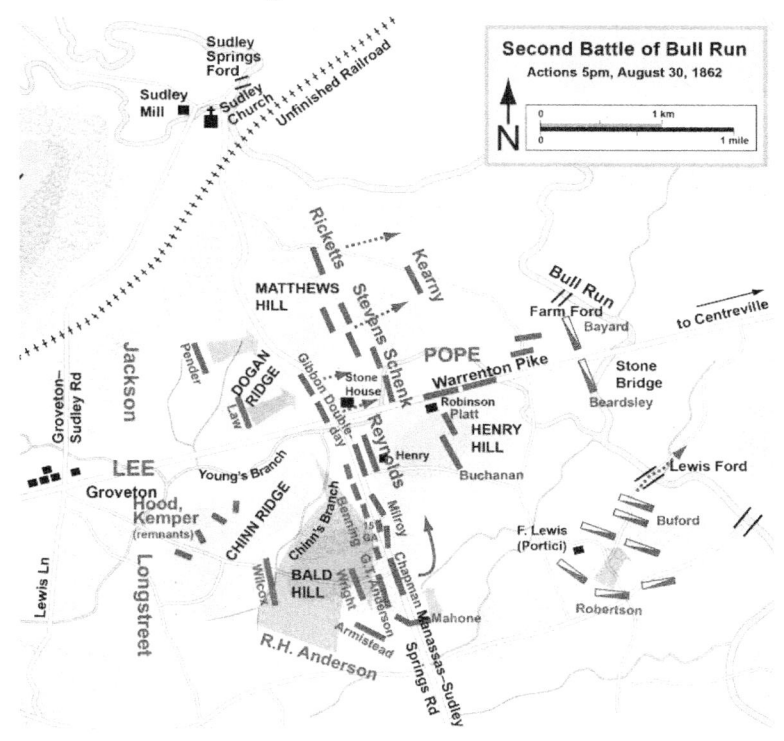

[5] Arrangement of troops at 5 p.m. on Saturday, August 30th, 1862, during the second day of the two-day-long Battle of Second Manassas, showing the approach of the Confederate forces pushing the Union against the Bull Run River and forcing them to retreat.

Pope's reluctance to create a safety net for his withdrawing troops now became a necessity. The enemy was upon them in vast numbers, and they intended to block their escape route, not only from the battlefield but also from Washington, DC. Pope, from his headquarters near Dogan Ridge, had been preoccupied with intelligence that McClellan's promised troops had finally arrived. Commanding General Halleck had informed Pope that not only was the Army of the Potomac's 2nd and 6th Corps at his disposal but also an additional corps, the 4th. (McClellan had, however, been ordered to remain in Washington—the glory would all belong to Pope!) But it was too late. Pope's men were being routed from the field as he read the belated news.

A flimsy Union line of defense was used on Chinn Ridge (southwest of the intersection of Warrenton Turnpike and Sudley Road) to allow time for Pope, with the help of McDowell and Kearny, to build a real defense along Sudley Road and on Henry House Hill (southeast of the intersection and the site of the First Battle of Manassas). McLean was the first on Chinn Ridge to meet the enemy, and he had aligned his four regiments of 1,200 men and one small battery west toward the tide of Confederate troops. McLean was aided by another Federal artillery battery positioned north of the turnpike. Confederate Brigadier General Shanks, in support of Hood, rushed up the left flank of the ridge, but he was repelled by McLean. The Union line held, for the time being, giving Pope half an hour to get reinforcements to the heat of battle.

Pope sacrificed unit after unit while he bought time to establish his defense. All the while, the Federals were subjected to the "Rebel yell" (a loud roar adopted by the Southerners during the war) as they closed on the ridge. General Lee had withheld three divisions to take Henry House Hill, but night was falling, and Longstreet's troops were becoming tired and disorganized. Two of these three divisions were a distance from the battlefield, including General Richard Anderson's reserves. The third division under David R. Jones (1825-1863, a career army officer who joined the Confederacy in the Civil War and died of natural causes during the war) arrived fresh to join the mob on Chinn Ridge and push the Northerners back. At 5 p.m., Lee dispatched Fighting Dick Anderson's troops from Brawner's Farm to join the fighting. These three thousand new troops could have easily overrun the exhausted Northerners, and they almost did along the southern line of fighting where the Union was falling back. It was a crucial opportunity for the Southerners to take Henry House Hill, but they lacked coordination and discipline. In addition, Anderson curiously withheld their advance (the reasons for this reluctance never became clear).

The Union had by now managed to establish themselves in a defensive line along the upper eastern bank of Sudley Road. They unleashed musket fire on the Southerners, who stalwartly continued to advance under Colonel George T. Anderson's Georgia regiment. With Anderson's command to "Knock hell out of those blue shirts!" the Georgia regiment stumbled forward, but the Union line held. The enemy was within forty-six meters (fifty yards) of the Union line and continued to be pelted with musket and heavy artillery fire. But the Rebel Army pushed forward relentlessly. In places, the Confederates pushed through the Union line, and the Federal troops rushed forward to seal the breach.

By 6 p.m. that evening, Union forces under Colonel John Kolte made a final effort to push back the Southerners and recapture a battery that had been lost on Chinn Ridge. But Longstreet's men conquered and dominated Chinn Ridge and Bald Hill after almost two hours of the most intense fighting of Second Manassas. However, the Confederates' goal of Henry House Hill was unlikely to be realized since their numbers were heavily depleted, their troops exhausted, their ammunition low, and night almost upon them. Many of the Federals had moved or were moving to safety across Bull Run and into Fairfax County toward the Union stronghold of Centreville. They were greatly aided by the spirited defense on Henry House Hill by Reynolds's Pennsylvania Reserves and Brigadier General George Sykes's 2nd Division. Altogether, Pope had at least created a line of defense of four brigades along the western slope of Henry House Hill to both deter the enemy and protect his withdrawing troops. The

Confederates had won the day's struggle, but their hopes of obliterating the Yankees were proving unlikely.

Darkness was falling when the Rebels managed to maneuver around the southern end of the enemy lines, and they were potentially in a position to begin a pincer-like flanking move upon the Union's left. General Jeb Stuart instructed the commander in charge, General Lewis Armistead (1817-1863, a career US Army officer who became a brigadier general in the Confederate Army but was killed the following year in the Battle of Gettysburg), to advance and envelop the exposed enemy line. But Armistead refused, citing darkness and heavy smoke as too confusing an environment in which to continue a fight—his men would not be able to tell friend from foe. Thus, the Confederate advance was temporarily halted.

Meanwhile, Jackson was pointing his artillery at the Yankees' direct line of withdrawal and began pelting the Union's right flank at 6 p.m., north of Henry House Hill. By 7 p.m., Pope had managed to establish a solid line of defense against Jackson. The Union held their defensive position until nightfall, but Pope understood the futility of continuing the fight and withdrew his remaining troops under cover of night, beginning about 8 p.m.

The final engagement of Second Manassas was a battle at about 7 p.m. between two cavalry units at Lewis Ford, south of Stone Bridge. Brigadier General Beverly Robertson (1827-1910, a career cavalry officer who changed allegiance for the Civil War) and Colonel Thomas Lafayette "Tex" Rosser (1836-1910, a cavalry officer and engineer who went back to serving the US after the war who was heralded by Jeb Stuart for his daring cavalry raids and tactical brilliance) of the Confederate cavalry under Jeb Stuart aimed to cut off the Union retreat by crossing Bull Run at Lewis Ford to encircle the enemy's rear. However, they were met by Union Brigadier General John Buford Jr's cavalry, which had superior numbers (Buford, 1826-1863, a career US Army cavalry officer, distinguished himself during the Battle of Gettysburg on July 1st, 1863). The fierce ten-minute encounter resulted in severe casualties on both sides, particularly amongst the leadership (with Buford being shot in the knee), but the Federal withdrawal was ultimately protected.

Leaving a line of decoy troops at the front, Pope hurriedly removed the remainder of his men, most of whom had crossed the Bull Run River by 11 p.m. The famous Stone Bridge over the Bull Run River along the Warrenton Turnpike had been destroyed by the Confederates in March of 1862, but a wooden one was rebuilt by the Union shortly after. Stone Bridge had proved a pivotal point during the First Battle of Bull Run, and when Pope withdrew his troops after the Second Battle of Bull Run, the Union destroyed the wooden bridge in their wake to prevent an easy Southern crossing. Pope's army retreated to the Federal stronghold of Centreville in failure and humiliation, just as General McDowell had done a year before. Admittedly, in 1862, the Union was in better shape than they had been in 1861, and they at least retreated in a calm and orderly manner, which was not the case in First Manassas.

The equally exhausted Confederates, who were low on ammunition, did not pursue the Yankees in the darkness. Lee telegrammed Confederate President Jefferson Davis after the battle, saying, "This army achieved today on the plains of Manassas a signal victory over the combined forces of Generals McClellan and Pope." For the Yankees, although technically the battle had unfolded behind enemy lines (in Southern territory), the area around Manassas in northeastern Virginia was largely under Union control for the Civil War, so the odds were significantly in favor of the Northerners. But the Rebels, using solid tactical maneuvers, exemplary timing, clear and steady commandeering, and unwavering resistance (so common of the Southerners), had once again won the day on the fateful grounds of Manassas.

Chapter 5 – Outcome of the Battle of Second Manassas

Amongst the multitude of General Pope's bad decisions before and during the Battle of Second Manassas, one question remains unanswered, and it's whether the tide could have turned in favor of the Union on Sunday, August 31st, had the Union remained in place to fight another day. Nightfall ended the events on Saturday 30th, and Pope had withdrawn his troops to save them from further suffering, but the Union had held the high ground at the end of the fighting on Saturday and also had three fresh corps from McClellan waiting near Centreville. There is a chance—given their higher numbers of fighting men and greater reinforcements of ammunition and artillery—that they could have regrouped and given the Confederates a beating.

On the Confederate side, Lee had given in to both Jackson and Longstreet at several points during the lead-up to and throughout Second Manassas, although he was technically the commanding general. Lee had reluctantly allowed Jackson's wild two-day flanking maneuver north to Bristoe Station and had relented to Longstreet's refusal to join the fight on August 29th. Although both instances of leeway were successful for the Confederates, this insubordination proved problematic later in the war when Lee struggled to control his headstrong generals to the detriment of his army.

The Union withdrawal from the battlefield at Second Bull Run did not officially end the fighting of the Confederate's northern Virginia campaign. Lee pressed his point and sent Jackson's exhausted troops to encircle Pope at Centreville and cut off their route back to Washington, DC. Thankfully, some of the Union cavalry detected the new enemy movement and alerted Pope to the approach, who was prepared. In the late afternoon of September 1st, some of Pope's forces intercepted the flanking wing of Jackson's, which had been sent to prevent the Union retreat to the Northern capital.

The enemy columns met at Ox Hill near Chantilly Plantation on the Little River Turnpike, eight kilometers (five miles) east of Centreville on the main road back to DC (thirty-four kilometers, or twenty-one miles, west of the capital). Jackson's divisions fought against two Union divisions under Major Generals Philip Kearny and Isaac Stevens, who were both sadly killed in the fighting. The Battle of Chantilly took place during a torrential thunderstorm—strangely reminiscent of the rainstorms of "Black Monday" after the Battle of First Manassas a year earlier. The battle was inconclusive and ended prematurely because of the weather, but it allowed Pope's army time to retreat back to Washington, DC, in comparative safety. Chantilly was officially the final battle of Lee's northern Virginia campaign.

The culmination of the Second Battle of Bull Run resulted in 14,462 Union casualties, including 1,747 killed, 8,452 wounded, and 4,263 captured or missing. It was a stunning defeat, with the casualties representing approximately 20 percent of those on the field. The Confederates listed 7,298 casualties, of which 1,096 were killed and 6,202 wounded—an equally shocking 15 percent of the field.

After the failure at Bull Run, Pope was relieved of his command on September 12th, 1862, along with the disbanding of the Army of Virginia, which had existed for a brief two and a half months. Three days after the end of Second Bull Run, Pope was posted to the

Department of the Northwest, well out of the way of the "real" fight with the South. He was now responsible for Native American uprisings. However, he remained in service to the US government, returning as a key figure toward the end of the war. His Army of Virginia was merged into the Army of the Potomac, which included the three fighting divisions he had "borrowed" for Second Manassas.

McClellan was once again—albeit temporarily—in charge of the main Federal Army. McClellan was removed from the head of the main army in November in that year, 1862, due to ongoing disputes with President Abraham Lincoln regarding tactical decisions and other political derision. He was replaced by the reluctant Major General Ambrose Burnside.

However, the humiliated Pope, who was responsible for the Northern loss, did not humbly accept responsibility for his actions but transferred the blame to other, more popular leaders. He mostly attributed the defeat of Second Bull Run to General Porter, accusing him of insubordination. Porter was subsequently arrested, court-martialed in November 1862, found guilty in January 1863, and dismissed from the military on January 21st in disgrace. Porter's open hostility toward Pope and the removal of his advocate, McClellan, from the military did not aid his cause. (McDowell is purported to have spoken against Porter in the hearing, potentially to save his own career.) Porter would spend many years defending himself against the official accusation of disobedience and misconduct. Fifteen years later, in 1878, a special commission exonerated Porter, confirming that his refusal to attack Longstreet resulted in a better, less damaging result for the Army of Virginia. His sentence was rescinded, as well as his dismissal from the army (although he officially resigned two days after being acquitted). Confederate commentator, Edward Porter Alexander (1835-1910), who served the Confederacy during the war as a brigadier general, wrote of Porter's dismissal, saying that the Confederates who knew Porter admired him greatly and considered his dismissal "one of the best fruits of their victory."

The Northern defeat at the Second Battle of Bull Run emboldened General Lee to continue with his campaign into enemy territory, and within the first week of September 1862, his troops splashed across the Potomac River into western Maryland. At this point, the Union was losing the war. The Maryland campaign continued through the first three weeks of September, with the campaign including the Battles of Harpers Ferry, South Mountain, and Antietam. Lee's real objective was the rail center of Harrisburg in Pennsylvania, approximately 193 kilometers (120 miles) north of Washington, DC. However, Lee and his army were repelled after the Battle of Antietam (also known as the Battle of Sharpsburg) on September 17th, 1862. After Antietam, Lee withdrew from Maryland back across the Potomac, and the Maryland (and effectively the summer) campaign ended. The Union forces did not pursue General Lee and the Confederates south. By the end of September 1862, the area around Manassas Railroad Junction was firmly back under Union control.

Conclusion

The Yankees' staggering loss at Second Bull Run not only allowed General Lee to penetrate the Union states and threaten the capital but also brought the fight to the world stage. The Southerners were garnering international recognition for their cause, which could have led to both political support and funding from abroad and a far more virulent enemy for the Union. The Confederacy knew that with their smaller numbers and more vulnerable tactical position, they could never win the war alone, so they were essentially playing a delaying game, keeping the Union at bay until foreign intervention arrived. The formation of the Confederate States of America had been largely based upon their belief that their cotton, and therefore the preservation of their slave-driven plantations, was invaluable to Europe.

It was clear that the US government, while holding command politically and administratively in most of the country, was weak militarily—mostly due to poor choices in field leadership. The fiery temperaments and passionate, planned, and decisive actions of the Southern generals overwhelmed the weak bureaucratic decisions made in the North, which then leaked onto the battlefields of the Civil War. The Union was contributing to their own demise.

The events surrounding the Battle of Second Manassas and the infringement by General Lee into Maryland and Pennsylvania meant that the North was losing the war, but the South was making assumptions that did not hold true. The Confederate government had never been legally recognized by its parent federal government nor diplomatically acknowledged as independent by any foreign country. The Southerners assumed that the international demand for their cotton would bring a multitude of European countries to their aid, which never happened. (The main countries to import Southern cotton were England and France, and neither were prepared to go to war with the US over the Confederacy's demands.)

In the Western Theater, the Union had made greater gains, and, technically, the various failures in the Eastern Theater from 1861 to 1862 were "inconclusive" since no permanent invasion of enemy ground on either side unfolded. A month after the Battle of Second Manassas, on September 22nd, 1862, President Lincoln issued the Emancipation Proclamation, which declared that all slaves held in the Confederacy were now freed. Until this point, abolition had been a tacit cause for the Civil War; now, for the South at least, it was a reality.

Lee's brief soirée into Northern territory in the autumn of 1862 that completed the Maryland campaign ended in a stalemate at the bloodiest one-day battle of the war—the Battle of Antietam—on September 17th. The Rebels could go no farther north and were forced to retreat. The US president grabbed the opportunity to nail his Emancipation Proclamation to their retreating backs. The European countries that the Confederacy were so dependent upon for support had abolished slavery decades beforehand, and they relied heavily on the US for other imports, including a quarter of their food. Help from Europe would not come—the Confederacy were on their own. With this knowledge and in the certainty that they could muster more military might and resources than the divided and isolated South, the US government was now in control. They simply needed to patiently play the tactical waiting game so familiar to the South until their foes eventually ran out of resources.

Here's another book by Captivating History that you might like

THE BATTLE OF ANTIETAM

A CAPTIVATING GUIDE TO AN IMPORTANT BATTLE OF THE AMERICAN CIVIL WAR

CAPTIVATING HISTORY

Free Bonus from Captivating History (Available for a Limited time)

Hi History Lovers!

Now you have a chance to join our exclusive history list so you can get your first history ebook for free as well as discounts and a potential to get more history books for free! Simply visit the link below to join.

Captivatinghistory.com/ebook

Also, make sure to follow us on Facebook, Twitter and Youtube by searching for Captivating History.

References

Battlefields,org:
Second Manassas, Second Bull Run, Brawner's Farm,
https://www.battlefields.org/learn/civil-war/battles/second-manassas, accessed June, July 2021.

Britannica.com:
Second Battle of Bull Run, https://www.britannica.com/event/Second-Battle-of-Bull-Run-1862, accessed June, July 2021.

Historynet.com:
Second Battle of Bull Run, https://www.historynet.com/second-battle-of-bull-run, accessed June, July 2021.

National Park Service:
Battle of Second Manassas (Second Bull Run), February 2011,
https://www.nps.gov/mana/learn/historyculture/second-manassas.htm, accessed June, July 2021,

Civil War Series, The Second Battle of Manassas, Section 1-7,
https://www.nps.gov/parkhistory/online_books/civil_war_series/18/sec7.htm, accessed June, July 2021.

Townsend, Jan, 2011, Ed. Burgess, James. *The Civil War in Prince William County.*, Prince William County Historical Commission, accessed via Prince William County Government, https://www.pwcva.gov/assets/documents/planning/HistComm_Book_The_Civil_War_in_PWC.pdf, June 2021.

TravelBrains.com:
Travelbrains Second Manassas Expedition Guide, accessed via AmericanCivilWar.com, https://americancivilwar.com/manassas2_travelbrains.html, June, July 2021.

Weapons and Warfare: History and Hardware of Warfare:
Lee Divides and Conquers at the Second Battle of Bull Run, https://weaponsandwarfare.com/2017/10/22/lee-divides-and-conquers-at-the-second-battle-of-bull-run/, accessed June, July 2021.

Wikipedia.com:
A.P. Hill's Light Division, https://en.wikipedia.org/wiki/A._P._Hill%27s_Light_Division, accessed June, July 2021,

American Civil War, https://en.wikipedia.org/wiki/American_Civil_War, accessed June, July 2021,

Battle of Cedar Mountain, https://en.wikipedia.org/wiki/Battle_of_Cedar_Mountain, accessed June, July 2021,

Emancipation Proclamation, https://en.wikipedia.org/wiki/Emancipation_Proclamation, accessed June, July 2021,

Fitz John Porter, https://en.wikipedia.org/wiki/Fitz_John_Porter, accessed June, July 2021,

Iron Brigade, https://en.wikipedia.org/wiki/Iron_Brigade, accessed June, July 2021,

John Gibbon, https://en.wikipedia.org/wiki/John_Gibbon, accessed June, July 2021,

John Pope,
htttps://en.wikipedia.org/wiki/John_Pope_(military_officer)#Civil_War, accessed June, July 2021,

Northern Virginia Campaign,
https://en.wikipedia.org/wiki/Northern_Virginia_campaign, accessed June, July 2021,

Peninsula Campaign,
https://en.wikipedia.org/wiki/Peninsula_campaign, accessed June, July 2021,

Rufus King,
https://en.wikipedia.org/wiki/Rufus_King_(general)#Civil_War, accessed June, July 2021,

Second Battle of Bull Run,
https://en.wikipedia.org/wiki/Second_Battle_of_Bull_Run, accessed June, July 2021.

Image References

[1] Northern Virginia Campaign, *Source:* Jespersen, Hal, 2011. Accessed via https://www.cwmaps.com/, https://www.cwmaps.com/freemaps/Northern_Virginia_Campaign_August_1862.png, June, July 2021.

[2] Second Bull Run, August 28, *Source:* Jespersen, Hal, 2011. Accessed via https://www.cwmaps.com/,, https://www.cwmaps.com/freemaps.html, June, July 2021.

[3] Second Bull Run, August 29, 12h00, *Source:* Jespersen, Hal, 2011. Accessed via https://www.cwmaps.com/, https://www.cwmaps.com/freemaps/Second_Bull_Run_Aug29_1200.png, June, July 2021.

[4] Second Bull Run, August 30, 15h00, *Source:* Jespersen, Hal, 2011. Accessed via https://www.cwmaps.com/, https://www.cwmaps.com/freemaps/Second_Bull_Run_Aug30_1500.png, June, July 2021.

[5] Second Bull Run, August 30, 17h00, *Source:* Jespersen, Hal, 2011. Accessed via https://www.cwmaps.com/, https://www.cwmaps.com/freemaps/Second_Bull_Run_Aug30_1700.png, June, July 2021.

Printed in Great Britain
by Amazon